Discovering Nature

A Journal
with a Selection of Quotes

A Division of Dharma Enterprises

1241 21st Street
Oakland, CA 94607
(510) 839-3931

Introduction:

As we were working on another project, a book on the power of nature and the spirit of beauty, gradually nature came to life: taking time to look, sitting still with a tree, looking at the shapes of shrubs, and seeing the tiny delicate forms of a flower piercing into space, something shifted. It was like becoming equal partners with nature; not even inner dialogues about what was observed, mere presence and intimacy.

When we were thinking about a title for this journal, this is what came to mind:

☆ The power of nature
☆ Exploring nature
☆ Look into nature
☆ Communicating with nature
☆ Reverence for nature
☆ Be nourished by nature
☆ In harmony with nature

Most of all what we liked was the process and satisfaction of discovering nature.

This journal is intended to start such a process for others, and deepen the natural-ness of being in nature. It feels so normal. Everything comes to life.

In this journal you will find a mixture of quotes from people who love nature, and simple suggestions for how to discover our natural relationship with nature.

All quotes and photographs are from *Mandala Gardens* (Amber Lotus, © 1991), unless otherwise specified. All exercises are from Amber Lotus' *Meditation Cards* sets "Opening to Nature" and "Inviting Beauty into Our Lives" (© 1993).

"The world of nature speaks to the human heart directly: We find ourselves already surrounded by beauty.

"Without any commentary or explanation, we can walk through a garden and feel the fullness of the experience. Colors and shapes delight the eyes, fragrance pours forth and enters our being as though we were drinking nectar. Sensations impress themselves upon the heart, communicating to human consciousness.

"Sustained, nourished, and supported by beauty, the heart begins to open, like the petals of a flower unfolding. When the heart opens, we begin to realize the unity of existence and our communion with nature.

"Cherishing beauty is the secret key to opening the heart, and once the heart opens, compassion and caring flow forth naturally. Thus, the world of nature has a crucial role to play in the development of the human values of compassion, love, and kindness."

"Every human being has a sacred duty to protect the welfare of our Mother Earth, from whom all life comes. In order to do this we must recognize the enemy—the one within us. We must begin with ourselves ... We must stand together, the four sacred colors of man, as the one family that we are in the interest of peace ..."

Leon Shenandoah, Tadodaho Chief

◇ Observe as much as possible in nature.

You may like to go for a walk and tell yourself everything you observe, in detail. Start out with a larger perspective, what you see while you walk; gradually go into more detail, and eventually sit down and look around you.

Finally, look at the earth immediately around you. Notice the shapes of grass and weeds, and all the animal activity. Try to observe details without interpretations.

"Commonly we stride through the out-of-doors too swiftly to see more than the most obvious and prominent things. For observing nature, the best pace is a snail's pace."

Edwin Way Teale

◇ Feel the earth you sit on; sit as though you have been sitting there for a long time, and will remain there for a long time.

"Let the children walk with Nature, let them see the beautiful blendings and communions of death and life, their joyous inseparable unity ... and they will learn that death is stingless indeed, and as beautiful as life, and that the grave has no victory, for it never fights."

John Muir

◇ While you are in nature, be aware of the sky,
   feel the warmth of the sunlight;
   let yourself be refreshed by the breeze.

"There is nature in all things."
American proverb

"Heaven is eternal, the Earth everlasting.
How come they to be so?
It is because they do not foster their own lives; that is why they live so long."

Tao Te Ching

◇ Observe nature. While sitting or walking around, by yourself or with others, notice shapes and forms, colors and smells, sounds and silence. First general impressions, then details—from the shapes of mountains and trees to branches, flowers, and blades of grass. Write down or share with others what you observe in detail.

The more you observe, the more will come alive.

◇ Listen to sounds, feel the air, let your fingers touch the ground and your immediate environment.

Emphasize "feeling" and "senses"; no need to have inner dialogues about your experience.

"The more you appreciate nature,
the more beauty you discover."

◇ While sitting still and being quiet, sense the vibrancy of colors, see the different shades of light. Notice distinct forms. Notice the space around forms. There is no need to interpret what you experience. Simply observe and sense.

Likewise with fragrances, tastes, and sounds. Listen to sounds. Listen to the silence within sound. No interpretations, just hearing sounds, smelling fragrances, tasting, and touching textures.

◇ Try to cultivate the feeling and taste of experience,
let it flow to the heart center.
You will feel nourished and more at ease;
you will feel stable and well balanced.

◇ The senses can provide food for the heart.
When we know how to nourish the heart through the senses, our being can unfold.

"The food of the soul is light and space."
Herman Melville

◇ Lie down on your stomach, close your eyes, and rest your head on one cheek. Spread your arms sideways on the ground. Imagine that you breathe in from deep in the earth, into your heart area, circulating the breath through the body, and breathing out from your navel back into the earth. Imagine that it is possible to have this cycle of breathing take place. Continue the circulation of breath for a while, then let yourself go. (For this exercise, you might like to cover yourself with a blanket.)

"Nature, time, and patience are the three great physicians."
English proverb

◇ Some time in the morning or late afternoon, you may like to lie on your back. Take some deep breaths, and imagine with each exhalation that you sink into the ground, until you feel grounded, part of the earth. Then open your eyes softly and look at the deep, blue sky. Imagine that you could breathe in the depth and the blueness of the sky. Let your awareness merge with the deep, blue sky. After a while, close your eyes, deeply relax, and let yourself go.

◇ Become aware of the sunlight. Notice how everything is illuminated by the sunlight. During the day, the light and the warmth of the sun make everything grow. Feel the warmth of the sun, how it warms your body. Gently look around and see light everywhere.

◇ Establish some relationship with water, rivers, lakes, and oceans. Our body is primarily made up of water.

Sit at the bank of a stream or river, facing the downstream direction. Imagine that the river goes through your lower back, flushing and cleansing you, and leaving the body in the front. Let your awareness merge with the sound and the current of the stream.

"If you live in the river, you should make friends with the crocodile."

Indian Proverb

◇ Try to spend some time near a lake or close to the ocean. The experiences are so different from one another. At the lake, there is an opportunity to become calm as we let our eyes gaze onto the smooth surface of the lake. We can let our minds merge with the stillness of the lake and, eventually, merging too with the light reflecting on the surface of the lake; our minds become still, and the distinction between past, present, and future seems to dissolve.

◇ The ocean front can be very energizing at the beginning. Seeing the movement and currents, the foam of the waves, can energize us. The point of all these exercises is to merge your consciousness with the awareness of what is observed. Rather than having inner dialogues, let your mind merge with the sight and sound of the ocean.

"Observe always that everything is the result of change, and get used to thinking that there is nothing Nature loves so well as to change existing forms and make new ones like them."

Marcus Aurelius

◊ Wind—Become aware of the air you breathe and the wind that makes things move. Air supports all life, each new breath is a new life. Feel the air and wind; let it touch your awareness. Contact "air". Become aware of wind and air.

"Teach your children
What we have taught our children—
That the earth is our mother
Whatever befalls the earth
Befalls the sons and daughters of the earth.
If men spit upon the ground
They spit upon themselves."
      Chief Seattle

◇ You may observe the perfection, the intricacies of nature, and that nothing is the same; everything is uniquely participating in nature. Nothing is holding back, everything fully engaged, in a neutral kind of way.

"Nature gives what no man can take away."
English proverb

◇ Eyes can look outward or can receive seeing. Open your eyes to receive a plant or flower. Imagine that the plant or flower looks at you, you receive it looking at you. Then gently look back, while still receiving. Develop looking and receiving, equally. Two partners, looking at each other, and receiving each other. Look at the flower, and receive the flower looking at you, as if you are attentively listening to the flower, telling you its life story. Listen to what the flower has to tell you. Meanwhile, the flower will receive you, equally. Just be still. Let the separation between you and the flower melt: Two "beings" totally present with one another.

"Look! Look!
Look deep into nature
and you will understand everything."
   Einstein

"When Chuang Tzu was about to die, his disciples began planning a splendid funeral.

"But he said: 'I shall have heaven and earth for my coffin; the sun and moon will be the jade symbols hanging by my side; planets and constellations will shine as jewels all around me, and al beings will be present as mourners at the wake. What more is needed? Everything is amply taken care of!'"

   Taoist text

"What a thing it is to sit absolutely alone,
In the forest, at night, cherished by this
Wonderful, unintelligible,
Perfectly innocent speech,
The most comforting speech in the world,
The talk of the watercourse everywhere in the hollow!
Nobody started it, nobody is going to stop it.
It will talk as long as it wants, this rain,
As long as it talks I am going to listen."
    Thomas Merton

"If I spent enough time with the tiniest creature
—even a caterpillar—
I would never have to prepare a sermon.
So full of God
Is every creature."

Meister Eckhart

"Light is essential for our being to unfold.
Like flower petals spreading out in the sunlight,
the bud of the human heart opens to beauty,
while light transmits that beauty."

"The appreciation we develop for our natural world will help us find a more balanced, sane approach to ourselves. Treating nature with reverence and appreciation, we might learn to treat ourselves the same way."

"Beauty is here in the midst of our world, in the midst of our lives, inviting us to participate and communicate."

"Each flower, each bird offers unique features: no two roses, and no two robins are exactly alike. An infinite exhibition of beauty is spread out before us, an unending display of patterns, shapes, and colors. Freely offered to us, this beauty touches the human heart with a gentle invitation, almost a caress."

"Each individual shape and form speaks this sweet communication if we would only hear. Each one dances before us, manifesting its special qualities for our appreciation, if we would only look and see. This communication is a wonderment: It is our good fortune as human beings to be interconnected and deeply involved in this larger world. We might cherish and feel cherished in return."

"Cherishing beauty is the secret key to opening the heart."

"To discover nature, first it seems we need to learn how to pay attention, to see, to communicate, to respond."

◇ You may like to write down all the different animals you observe, the different birds in the sky and in the trees, the animals above the ground, such as deer, and then the animals on the ground. As you write down the animals noticed, you will discover more and more animals.

◇ Then stay with one animal or a group of animals. Observe their habits, and habitat. What strikes you most about the animal observed? And draw the animal in your note book. Notice how each animal of the same species is different; no two birds alike, no two spiders the same.

Each flower, each bird offers unique features: no two roses, and no two robins are exactly alike.

"Evidently, the Greeks also followed a custom similar to the Persian one of making youths plant trees:

Odysseus on his return home made himself known to his aged father, Laertes, by pointing out the trees which had been given to him as a child."

Julia S. Berrall

◇ When you are in your garden or neighborhood, observe
the colors and fragrances, the textures and forms; how the
different plants, shrubs, and trees are layered and form
worlds within worlds.

◇ Observe what is growing and what is doing well. The more we observe, the more the garden or neighborhood seems to come alive. Every morning or once a day, you may like to go around to see the changes. Eventually, you will have a relationship with everything in the garden or neighborhood and they will "inform you". Nature invites you to cherish and foster beauty.

"Consider that before long you will be nobody and nowhere, nor will any of the things exist which you now see, nor any of those who are now living. For all things are formed by nature to change and be turned and to perish in order that other things in continuous succession may exist."

Marcus Aurelius

"When you are crossing the desert, plant trees, for you may be coming back the same way in your old age when you will be glad of the shade".

Persian Proverb

"If you wish your children to think deep thoughts, to know the holiest emotions, take them to the woods and hills, and give them the freedom of the meadows; the hills purify those who walk on them".

Richard Jeffries

"Our relationship with nature offers us
two precious opportunities:
to receive beauty and to foster it."

"By protecting and preserving the field of beauty
that offers nourishment for the heart,
we serve the highest human values."

"If the realm of nature were to disappear, leaving us only the manufactured world of human making, our civilization could scarcely be called human."

◇ Whenever you make a new discovery, or you appreciate something specifically, like the opening of a flower, in your mind, share your experience with someone else: "if … *(name)* could see this." In sharing appreciation and beauty of nature, our mind will send ripples of joy.

"We could begin in our own backyard, creating a small garden, enjoying our favorite plants, watching each one grow. These simple plants can become friends that satisfy all our senses, offering us wonderful colors and shapes, subtle fragrances, delicious fruits and vegetables. Their substance even becomes part of our bodies, supporting our life and nourishing us like a mother."

"Recognizing the motherhood of nature, we might feel reverence, appreciation, and a desire for a deeper understanding of this unique relationship."